BECAUSE
WE'RE
FRIENDS

```
I0170970
```

AN OUTREACH RESOURCE
FROM
HEALTHY LIFE PRESS

Healthy Life Press
Orlando, Florida

FROM: _____

TO: _____

DATE: _____

BECAUSE WE'RE FRIENDS

Copyright © 2010, 2013 by Gary A. Burlingame, and
Healthy Life Press, 2603 Drake Drive, Orlando, FL 32810
www.healthylifepress.com

Printed in the United States of America
Internal photos by Gary Burlingame
Cover design by Judy Johnson

Burlingame, Gary A. (1958 -)

Because We're Friends

ISBN 978-1-9392-6712-2

1. Evangelism; 2. Christianity

Published by Healthy Life Press. Most Healthy Life Press resources are available worldwide through bookstores and on-
line outlets, depending on their format. This book also
exists in eBook format for all eBook readers, or as a down-
loadable and printable PDF from info@healthylifepress.com.

Multiple copy discounts may be arranged by contacting:
info@healthylifepress.com. Distribution of this book in any
format without prior written arrangement is a violation of
international copyright laws, and strictly prohibited.

Because we're friends ....

Can we talk about God?

IF being friends *DIDN'T* matter to me, I'd take the easy way out and *NOT* talk to you about God.

Far too often we avoid having difficult discussions with people we care about.

Let's not let that happen between us.

You and me, we're *friends*.

So, can you spare maybe 10 minutes?

That's all – nothing else.

Nothing to buy. No requirements.

Nothing you need to return to me.

Just a few pages to read and consider.

Can you spare the time?

What do friends do *best*?

We watch out for each other. If I find a great sale, I tell you. I don't drive to your house, insist that you get in the car, take you to the store, and pressure you into buying something on sale. Instead, I give you the information and let *you* decide.

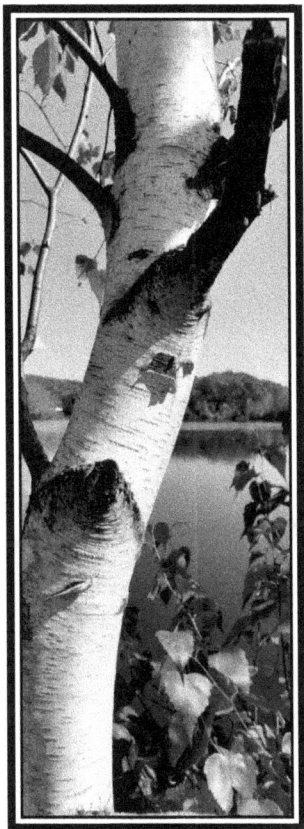

BUT if you wanted to go shopping together, you could give me a call and we'd go together.

This book is no different; I'm simply sharing something with you. Is that okay?

I respect your freedom

Whatever you decide, after reading this short book, we are still and will always be friends. That is why I am *not* in your face to argue about religion, or to pressure you into listening to me about the importance of true faith. You can decide whether you want to talk about it or leave it alone. The decision is always *yours* to make. I have made my decision and I am happy with it. I respect the freedom you have to make your own decision.

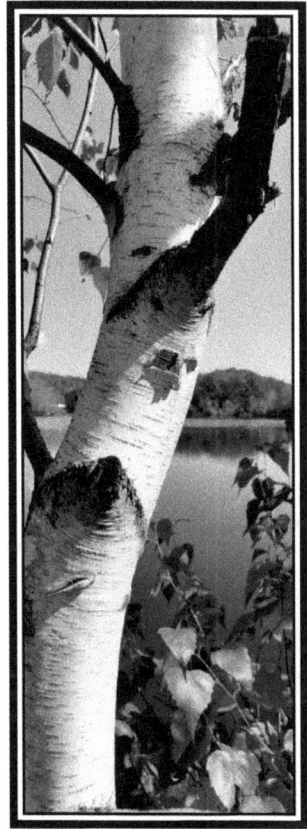

But why not decide to turn the page?

Too much bad info going around

Some people think that when you believe in God you have to give up the good things in life. I made *my* decision to believe and all I can say is I have *no* regrets. Anything I chose to give up was not worth the keeping! We all change as we get older. I bet you watch different movies, read different books, and listen to different music than when you were a kid.

You changed! Was it difficult? Or did it just happen naturally?

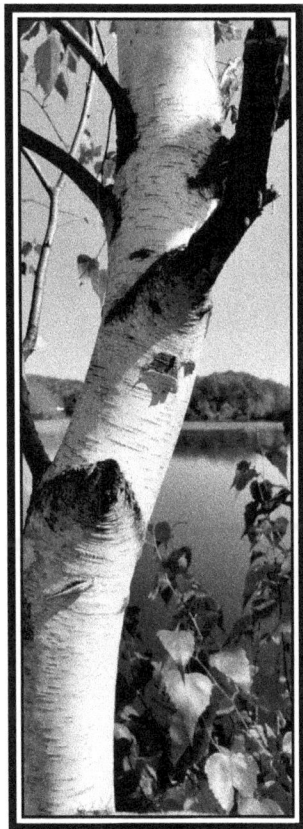

God makes sense

My only reason *NOT* to believe in God comes from the pressure people put on me. It does not come from logic or experience or science. Faith makes sense out of many things. Faith *is* a necessary part of life, more than most of us like to think. We take steps of faith every day. When you jump, don't you have faith that you will come back down again? What guarantees that gravity will always be there?

What else do you have faith in? Please, give it some thought.

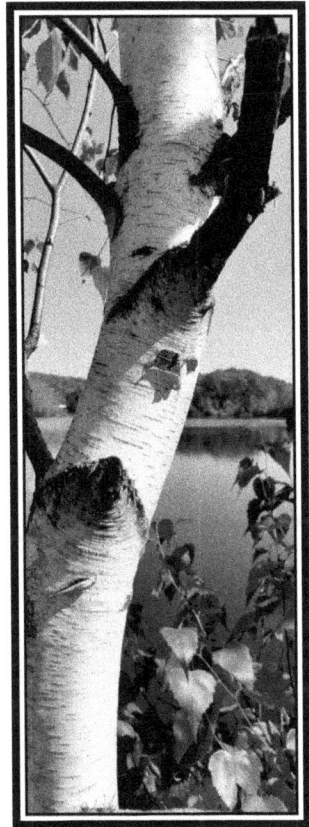

Do you *believe* in luck?

Some people call it chance. Some people say it's fate. You meet someone who knows someone else. You just miss being in an accident. Your eye catches something that you should have missed. Over and over throughout life, we experience things happening by coincidence or by chance, or by the hand of *something bigger* than us. If it happened only a few times a year, okay, call it chance. But it happens way too much for it to be chance.

Luck, chance, fate ... or the providence of God? Which do you choose to believe in?

What gives life meaning?

Do you really want to live in a world where God does not exist? Think about it and ask yourself some questions:
What motivates you to get out of bed every day?
Why be nice to someone?
Why should others be nice to you?
Why ask questions?
Why pursue truth?
Why explore the universe?
Why live a long life if it ends without meaning?

God provides answers to *all* these questions. All you have to do is ask.

Just look around you

Sometimes we get so used to seeing or hearing something that we forget it's there. When I look around at the sky, the trees, the insects, the birds, the sea and the universe I see something *bigger* than me out there. And just look at your own body. Aren't you amazed that the microscopic mechanisms and cell functions work every second of every day without failing? Can you buy a car, watch, or computer that works that well? Who designed us to work like this?

There must be more to it…….
Why not ask?

If you
DO
believe...

Then WHO is that God? What do you believe in? Why believe in something you don't know?

Why cheer for a sports team without knowing who is on the team or what game they are playing?

How do you relate to God? What does He expect from you? Some people reject God because they have a wrong view of Him, not because they know Him.

People judge God on things He never said or did. Does that make sense?

Let's go one step deeper

The name of Jesus causes controversy. Yes, some people curse His name. Some people never want it mentioned in public. Why is *Jesus* such a problem? He was a man who really lived. *Everyone* believes that! We know that Jesus lived as surely as we know that the pharaohs lived who built the great pyramids. The evidence and proof are there. The man Jesus *really lived.* But He was *more than* just a man! That's the sticky part.

Yet why is that such a problem for some people?

We listen to gossip

When I want to know Jesus, I don't make things up in my head or listen to loose talk. I go to the Bible and read for myself what God said about Jesus or what Jesus Himself said. If I want to know something about you, wouldn't you want me to listen directly to you rather than hear what others have to say? Yet too often we listen to gossip about Jesus. All I suggest is that you go to the source and see for yourself what it says. Stop listening to rumors. Get the facts straight.

And if you need help, please ask.

There's a lot to learn

There are lots of study books, Bibles and web sites you can tap into to learn about God and Jesus.

I do this constantly. I don't have the ability to become an expert in Bible knowledge or history, so I read books and I read the Bible and I listen to sermons.

Web sites are also available but like anything on the Internet, we have to be careful which sites we go to. It's not that hard to find good books.

If I can help, please ask.

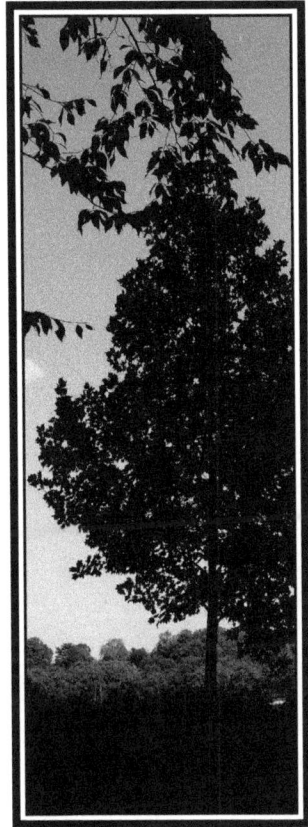

You are *never* alone!

Church is where God's people practice helping each other. It is not a perfect place, nor does it have perfect people. It is where people agree on one thing – that *Jesus* is their source of truth and hope and peace. It's quite wonderful, really, that Jesus would be so patient with us (through His helping Spirit) to teach us to be kind, hospitable, gentle and encouraging to one another. This is the type of community in which we grow to be healthy: mentally, emotionally, and spiritually.

If you want help finding a church, please ask.

Does death worry you?

I dislike talking about life insurance. Some call it a necessary evil. But I know that if I care about my family, I will take care of my life insurance.

Did you ever think about after-life insurance? I believe that God didn't set us up to live and die and that's it. I believe there is a spiritual world and that heaven *really* exists.

The fact that we will all die someday does not have to leave us feeling hopeless.

We *can live* with a purpose that brings joy and hope to life.

Are we friends, or just faking it?

I'm not faking it!

We *are* friends.

If you want to talk, let me know.

Just ask.

No pressure.

Tomorrow or next week or years from now . . . . . ANY time is fine with me.

But whatever you choose to do, we're friends and I *still* care about you!

Great discoveries come to people who are not afraid to ask questions.

The start to getting an answer *is* a question.

Please ask.

Some Churches to Check Out

_____

_____

_____

_____

_____

BIBLES & STUDY GUIDES TO HELP YOU

_____

_____

_____

_____

_____

Some Additional Books to Read

_____

_____

_____

_____

_____

Some Web Sites to Check Out

_____

_____

_____

_____

_____

CHRISTIAN MUSIC YOU MIGHT ENJOY

_____

_____

_____

_____

_____

Resources from
Healthy Life Press

We've Got Mail: The New Testament Letters in Modern English – As Relevant Today as Ever! by Rev. Warren C. Biebel, Jr. – A modern English paraphrase of the New Testament Letters, sure to inspire in readers a loving appreciation for God's Word. (Printed book: $9.95; PDF eBook: $6.95; together: $15.00; commercial eBook reader version: $9.99.)

Hearth & Home – Recipes for Life, by Karey Swan (7th Edition) – Far more than a cookbook, this classic is a life book, with recipes for life as well as for great food. Karey describes how to buy and prepare from scratch a wide variety of tantalizing dishes, while weaving into the book's fabric the wisdom of the ages plus the recipe that she and her husband used to raise their kids. A great gift for Christmas or for a new bride. (Perfect Bound Version (8 x 10, glossy cover): $17.95; PDF eBook version: $12.95; Together as set: $24.95; commercial eBook reader version: $9.99.)

Who Me, Pray? Prayer 101: Praying Aloud, for Beginners, by Gary A. Burlingame – *Who Me, Pray?* is a practical guide for prayer, based on Jesus' direction in "The Lord's Prayer," with examples provided for use in typical situations where you might be asked or expected to pray in public. (Printed book: $6.95 PDF eBook: $2.99; together: $7.95.)

The Big Black Book – What the Christmas Tree Saw, by Rev. Warren C. Biebel, Jr – An original Christmas story, from the perspective of the Christmas tree. This little book is especially suitable for parents to read to their children at Christmas time or all year-round. (Printed book: $7.95; PDF eBook: $4.95; Together: $10.95; commercial eBook reader version: $6.95.)

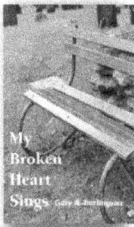

My Broken Heart Sings, the poetry of Gary Burlingame – In 1987, Gary and his wife Debbie lost their son Christopher John, at only six months of age, to a chronic lung disease. This life-changing experience gave them a special heart for helping others through similar loss and pain. (Printed book: $10.95; PDF eBook: $6.95; Together: $13.95; commercial eBook reader version: $9.99 at eChristian.com; Amazon.com; bn.com.)

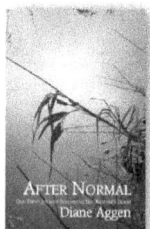

After Normal: One Teen's Journey Following Her Brother's Death, by Diane Aggen – Based on a journal the author kept following her younger brother's death. It offers helpful insights and understanding for teens facing a similar loss or for those who might wish to understand and help teens facing a similar loss. (Printed book: $11.95; PDF eBook: $6.95; together: $15.00; commercial eBook reader version: $8.99.)

In the Unlikely Event of a Water Landing – Lessons Learned from Landing in the Hudson River, by Andrew Jamison, MD. The author was flying standby on US Airways Flight 1549 toward Charlotte on January 15, 2009, from New York City, where he had been interviewing for a residency position. Little did he know that the next stop would be the Hudson River. Riveting and inspirational, this book would be especially helpful for people in need of hope and encouragement. (Printed book: $8.95; PDF eBook: $6.95; Together: $12.95; commercial eBook reader version: $8.99.)

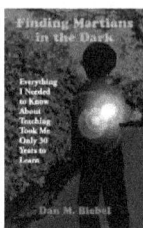

Finding Martians in the Dark – Everything I Needed to Know About Teaching Took Me Only 30 Years to Learn, by Dan M. Biebel – Packed with wise advice based on hard experience, and laced with humor, this book is a perfect teacher's gift year-round. Susan J. Wegmann, PhD, says, "Biebel's sardonic wit is mellowed by a genuine love for kids and teaching. . . . A Whitman-like sensibility flows through his stories of teaching, learning, and life." (Printed book: $10.95; PDF eBook: $6.95; Together: $15.00; commercial eBook: $9.99.)

Because We're Family and *Because We're Friends*, by Gary A. Burlingame – Sometimes things related to faith can be hard to discuss with your family and friends. These booklets are designed to be given as gifts, to help you open the door to discussing spiritual matters with family members and friends who are open to such a conversation. (Printed book: $5.95 each; PDF eBook: $4.95 each; together: $9.95 per pair [printed & eBook of the same title]; commercial eBook reader version: $5.95.)

The Transforming Power of Story: How Telling Your Story Brings Hope to Others and Healing to Yourself, by Elaine Leong Eng, MD, and David B. Biebel, DMin – This book demonstrates, through multiple true life stories, how sharing one's story, especially in a group setting, can bring hope to listeners and healing to the one who shares. Individuals facing difficulties will find this book greatly encouraging. (Printed book: $14.99; PDF eBook: $9.99; together: $19.99; commercial eBook reader version: $9.99.)

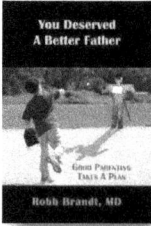

You Deserved a Better Father: Good Parenting Takes a Plan, by Robb Brandt, MD – About parenting by intention, and other lessons the author learned through the loss of his firstborn son. It is especially for parents who believe that bits and pieces of leftover time will be enough for their own children. (Printed book: $12.95 each; PDF eBook: $6.95; together: $17.95; commercial eBook reader version: $9.99.)

Jonathan, You Left Too Soon, by David B. Biebel, DMin

One pastor's journey through the loss of his son, into the darkness of depression, and back into the light of joy again, emerging with a renewed sense of mission. (Printed book: $12.95; PDF eBook: $5.99; together: $15.00 at healthylifepress.com.

The Spiritual Fitness Checkup for the 50-Something Woman, by Sharon V. King, PhD – Following the stages of a routine medical exam, the author describes ten spiritual fitness "checkups" midlife women can conduct to assess their spiritual health and tone up their relationship with God. Each checkup consists of the author's personal reflections, a Scripture reference for meditation, and a "Spiritual Pulse Check," with exercises readers can use for personal application. (Printed book: $8.95; PDF eBook: $6.95; together: $12.95.)

The Other Side of Life – Over 60? God Still Has a Plan for You, by Rev. Warren C. Biebel Jr. – Drawing on biblical examples and his 60-plus years of pastoral experience, Rev. Biebel helps older (and younger) adults understand God's view of aging and the rich life available to everyone who seeks a deeper relationship with God as they age. Rev. Biebel explains how to: Identify God's ongoing plan for your life; Rely on faith to manage the anxieties of aging; Form positive, supportive relationships; Cultivate patience; Cope with new technologies; Develop spiritual integrity; Understand the effects of dementia; Develop a Christ-centered perspective of aging. (Printed book: $10.95; PDF eBook: $6.95; together: $15.00; commercial eBook reader version: $9.99.)

My Faith, My Poetry by Gary A. Burlingame – This unique book of Christian poetry is actually two in one. The first collection of poems, *A Day in the Life*, explores a working parent's daily journey of faith. The reader is carried from morning to bedtime, from "In the Details," to "I Forgot to Pray," back to "Home Base," and finally to "Eternal Love Divine." The second collection of poems, *Come Running*, is wonder, joy, and faith wrapped up in words that encourage and inspire the mind and the heart. (Printed book: $10.95; PDF eBook: $6.95; together: $13.95; commercial eBook reader version: $9.99.)

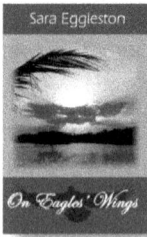

On Eagles' Wings, by Sara Eggleston – One woman's life journey from idyllic through chaotic to joy, carried all the way by the One who has promised to never leave us nor forsake us. Remarkable, poignant, moving, and inspiring, this autobiographical account will help many who are facing difficulties that seem too great to overcome or even bear at all. It is proof that Isaiah 40:31 is as true today as when it was penned, "But they that wait upon the LORD shall renew their strength; they shall mount up with wings as eagles; they shall run, and not be weary; and they shall walk, and not faint." (Printed book: $14.95; PDF eBook: $8.95; together: $22.95; commercial eBook reader version: $9.99.)

Richer Descriptions, by Gary A. Burlingame – A unique and handy manual, covering all <u>nine</u> human senses in seven chapters, for Christian speakers and writers. Exercises and a speaker's checklist equip speakers to engage their audiences in a richer experience. Writing examples and a writer's guide help writers bring more life to the characters and scenes of their stories. Bible references encourage a deeper appreciation of being created by God for a sensory existence. (Printed book: $15.95; PDF eBook: $8.95; together: $22.95; commercial eBook reader version: $9.99.)

Unless otherwise noted on the site itself, shipping is free for all products purchased through <u>*www.healthylifepress.com*</u>.

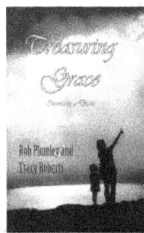

Treasuring Grace, by Rob Plumley and Tracy Roberts – *This novel was inspired by a dream.* Liz Swanson's life isn't quite what she'd imagined, but she considers herself lucky. She has a good husband, beautiful children, and fulfillment outside of her home through volunteer work. On some days she doesn't even notice the dull ache in her heart. While she's preparing for their summer kickoff at Lake George, the ache disappears and her sudden happiness is mistaken for anticipation of their weekend. However, as the family heads north, there are clouds on the horizon that have nothing to do with the weather. Only Liz's daughter, who's found some of her mother's hidden journals, has any idea what's wrong. But by the end of the weekend, there will be no escaping the truth or its painful buried secrets. Printed: $12.95; PDF eBook: $7.95; together: $19.95; commercial eBook reader version: $9.99.

Life's A Symphony, by Mary Z. Smith – When Kate Spence Cooper receives the news that her husband, Jack, has been killed in the war, she and her young son Jeremy move back to Crawford Wood, Tennessee to be closer to family. Since Jack's death Kate feels that she's lost trust in everyone, including God. Will she ever find her way back to the only One whom she can always depend upon? And what about Kate's match making brother, Chance? The cheeky man has other ideas on how to bring happiness into his sister's life once more. (Printed book: $12.95; PDF eBook: $7.95; together: $19.95; commercial eBook reader version: $9.99.)

Your Mind at Its Best – 40 Ways To Keep Your Brain Sharp by David B. Biebel, DMin; James E. Dill, MD; and, Bobbie Dill, RN – Everyone wants their mind to function at high levels throughout life. In 40 easy-to-understand chapters, readers will discover a wide variety of tips and tricks to keep their minds sharp. Synthesizing science and self-help, *Your Mind at Its Best* makes fascinating neurological discoveries understandable and immediately applicable to readers of any age. (Printed book: $13.99.)

From Orphan to Physician – The Winding Path, by Chun-Wai Chan, MD – From the foreword: "In this book, Dr. Chan describes how his family escaped to Hong Kong, how they survived in utter poverty, and how he went from being an orphan to graduating from Harvard Medical School and becoming a cardiologist. The writing is fluent, easy to read and understand. The sequence of events is realistic, emotionally moving, spiritually touching, heart-warming, and thought provoking. The book illustrates . . . how one must have faith in order to walk through life's winding path." (Printed book: $14.95; PDF eBook: $8.95; together: $22.95; commercial eBook reader version: $9.99.)

12 Parables, by Wayne Faust – Timeless Christian stories about doubt, fear, change, grief, and more. Using tight, entertaining prose, professional musician and comedy performer Wayne Faust manages to deal with difficult concepts in a simple, straightforward way. These are stories you can read aloud over and over—to your spouse, your family, or in a group setting. Packed with emotion and just enough mystery to keep you wondering, while providing lots of points to ponder and discuss when you're through, these stories relate the gospel in the tradition of the greatest speaker of parables the world has ever known, who appears in them often. (Printed book: $14.95; PDF eBook: $8.95; together: $22.95; commercial eBook reader version: $9.99.)

The Answer is Always "Jesus," by Aram Haroutunian, who gave children's sermons for 15 years at a large church in Golden, Colorado—well over 500 in all. This book contains 74 of his most unforgettable presentations—due to the children's responses. Pastors, homeschoolers, parents who often lead family devotions, or other storytellers will find these stories, along with comments about props and how to prepare and present them, an invaluable asset in reconnecting with the simplest, most profound truths of Scripture, and then to envision how best to communicate these so even a child can understand them.(Printed book: $12.95; PDF eBook: $8.95; together: $19.95; commercial eBook reader version: $9.99.)

New FROM HEALTHY LIFE PRESS
CHECK WEBSITE FOR DETAILS

The Secret of Singing Springs, by Monte Swan. One Colorado family's treasure-hunting adventure along the trail of Jesse James.

I AM – Transformed in Him, by Diana Burg and Kim Tapfer, a meditative women's Bible study of the I AM statements of Christ.

Nature-God's Second Book, by Elvy Rolle, who discovered true healing through immersing herself in God's beautiful Creation. In this full-color book (print/ePub) she shares her insights.

Handbook of Faith by Rev. Warren C. Biebel Jr. – The *New York Times World 2011 Almanac* claimed that there are 2 billion, 200 thousand Christians in the world, with "Christians" being defined as "followers of Christ." The original 12 followers of Christ changed the world; indeed, they changed the history of the world. So this author, a pastor with over 60 years' experience, poses and answers this logical question: "If there are so many 'Christians' on this planet, why are they so relatively ineffective in serving the One they claim to follow?" Answer: Because, unlike Him, they do not know and trust the Scriptures, implicitly. This little volume will help you do that. (Printed book: $8.95; PDF eBook: $6.95; together: $13.95; commercial eBook reader version: $8.95.)

Pieces of My Heart, by David L. Wood – Eighty-two lessons from normal everyday life. David's hope is that these stories will spark thoughts about God's constant involvement and intervention in our lives and stir a sense of how much He cares about every detail that is important to us. The piece missing represents his son, Daniel, who died in a fire shortly before his first birthday. (Printed book: $16.95; PDF eBook: $8.95; Set: $24.95; commercial eBook version: $9.99.)

PLEASE NOTE: Prices of resources listed in this catalog may have changed since these pages were printed. Current prices are available at: www.healthylifepress.com.

Dream House by Justa Carpenter – Written by a New England builder of several hundred homes, the idea for this book came to him one day as he was driving that came to him one day as was driving from one job site to another. He pulled over and recorded it so he would remember it, and now you will remember it, too, if you believe, as he does, that ". . . He who has begun a good work in you will complete it until the day of Jesus Christ." (Printed book: $8.95; PDF eBook: $6.95; Set: $13.95; commercial eBook reader version: $8.95.)

A Simply Homemade Clean, by homesteader Lisa Barthuly – "Somewhere along the path, it seems we've lost our gumption, the desire to make things ourselves," says the author. "Gone are the days of 'do it yourself.' Really . . . why bother? There are a slew of retailers just waiting for us with anything and everything we could need; packaged up all pretty, with no thought or effort required. It is the manifestation of 'progress' . . . right?" I don't buy that!" Instead, Lisa describes how to make safe and effective cleansers for home, laundry, and body right in your own home. This saves money and avoids exposure to harmful chemicals often found in commercially produced cleansers. (Printed book: $12.99; PDF eBook: $6.95; Set: $14.95; commercial eBook reader version: $8.95.)

Unless otherwise noted on the site itself, shipping is free for all products purchased through www.healthylifepress.com.

RECOMMENDED RESOURCES –
PRO-LIFE DVD SERIES

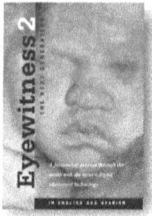

EYEWITNESS 2 (PUBLIC SCHOOL VERSION) – This DVD has been used in many public schools. It is a fascinating journey through 38 weeks of pregnancy, showing developing babies via cutting edge digital ultrasound technology. Separate chapters allow viewing distinct segments individually. (List Price: $34.95; Sale Price: $24.95.)

WINDOW TO THE WOMB (2 DVD DISC SET) Disc 1: Ian Donald (1910-1987) "A Prophetic Legacy;" Disc 2: "A Journey from Death To Life" (50 min) – Includes history of sonography and its increasing impact against abortion—more than 80% of expectant parents who "see" their developing baby choose for life. Perfect for counseling and education in Pregnancy Centers, Christian schools, homeschools, and churches. (List: $49.95; Sale: $34.95.)

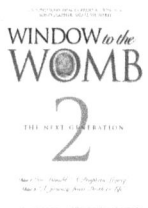

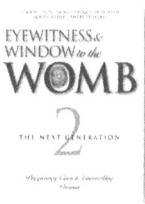

WINDOW TO the WOMB (PREGNANCY CARE & COUNSELING VERSION) – Facts about fetal development, abortion complications, post-abortion syndrome, and healing. Separate chapters allow selection of specialized presentations to accommodate the needs and time constraints of their situations. (List: $34.95; Sale: $24.95.)

RECOMMENDED RESOURCES – BOOKS

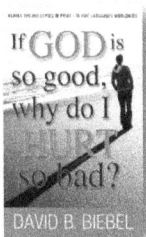

If God Is So Good, Why Do I Hurt So Bad?, by David B. Biebel, DMin – In this best-selling classic (over 200,000 copies in print worldwide, in five languages) on the subject of loss and renewal, first published in 1989, the author comes alongside people in pain, and shows the way through and beyond it, to joy again. This book has proven helpful to those who are struggling and to those who wish to understand and help. Revised and re-released July 2010. (Printed book: $12.95; PDF eBook: $8.95; Set: $19.95.)

52 Ways to Feel Great Today, by David B. Biebel, DMin, James E. Dill, MD, and Bobbie Dill, RN – **Increase Your Vitality, Improve your Outlook.** Simple, fun, inexpensive things you can do to increase your vitality and improve your outlook. Why live an "ordinary" life when you could be experiencing the extraordinary? Don't settle for good enough when "great" is such a short stretch away. Make today great! (Printed book: $14.99.)

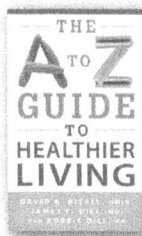

The A to Z Guide To Healthier Living, by David B. Biebel, DMin, James E. Dill, MD, and Bobbie Dill, RN – You'll find great info on: avoiding fad diets, being kind to your GI tract, building healthy bones, finding contentment, getting a good night's sleep, keeping your relationships strong, simplifying your life, staying creative, and much more. (Printed book: 12.99; commercial eBook versions: $8.99.)

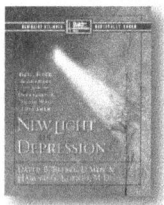

New Light on Depression, a CBA Gold Medallion winner, by David B. Biebel, DMin, and Harold Koenig, MD – The most exhaustive Christian resource on a subject that is more common than we might wish. Hope for those with depression and help for those who love them. (Printed book: $15.00.)

VOWS, a Romantic novel by F.F. Whitestone – When the police cruiser pulled up to the curb outside, Faith Framingham's heart skipped a beat, for she could see that Chuck, who should have been driving, was not in the vehicle. Chuck's partner, Sandy, stepped out slowly. Sandy's pursed lips and ashen face spoke volumes. Faith waited by the front door, her hands clasped tightly, to counter the fact that her mind was already reeling. "Love never fails." A compelling story. (Printed book: $12.99; full color PDF eBook: $9.99. Combination, only from publisher: $19.99. Other eReader options: BN.com and Amazon.com.)

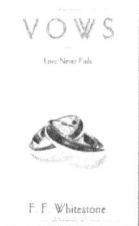

Our God Given Senses, by Gary A. Burlingame – Did you know humans have NINE senses? The Bible draws on these senses to reveal spiritual truth. We are to taste and see that the Lord is a good. We are to carry the fragrance of Christ. Our faith is produced upon hearing. Jesus asked Thomas to touch him. God created us for a sensory experience and that is what you will find in this book. (Printed book: $12.99; full color PDF eBook: $9.99; together: $19.99, direct from publisher; other eReader options: BN.com and Amazon.com. Available Spring 2013.)

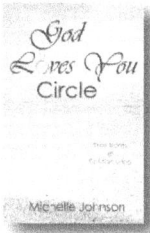

God Loves You Circle, by Michelle Johnson – Daily inspiration for your deeper walk with Christ. This collection of short stories of Christian living will make you laugh, make you cry, but most of all make you contemplate–the meaning and value of walking with the Master moment-by-moment, day-by-day. (Full-color printed book: $17.95, PDF eBook: $9.99; set $24.95, direct from publisher; eBook versions: $9.99, at eChristian.com; Amazon.com; BN.com.)

ABOUT HEALTHY LIFE PRESS

Healthy Life Press was founded with a primary goal of helping previously unpublished authors to get their works to market, and to reissue worthy, previously published works that were no longer available. Our mission is to help people toward optimal vitality by providing resources promoting physical, emotional, spiritual, and relational health as viewed from a Christian perspective. We see health as a verb, and achieving optimal health as a process—a crucial process for followers of Christ if we are to love the Lord with all our heart, soul, mind, AND strength, and our neighbors as ourselves—for as long as He leaves us here. We are a collaborative and cooperative small Christian publisher. We share the costs, we share the proceeds.

For information about publishing with us, e-mail: info@healthylifepress.com.

www.ingramcontent.com/pod-product-compliance
Lightning Source LLC
Chambersburg PA
CBHW060722030426
42337CB00017B/2975